Seeking the Lighthouse

Reflections for those travelling ...

by Wendy

Photographs by A... ...eery

Seeking the Lighthouse
Published, edited and distributed by TLM Trading Limited
www.tlmtrading.com

First Published 2012
© Text: Wendy Grant
© Photos: Adam Feery
www.adamfeeryphotography.co.uk

Wendy Grant has asserted her right to be identified as the author
of this work in accordance with the Copyright,
Designs and Patents Act, 1988
All rights and subsidiary rights have been granted to
The Leprosy Mission Trading Limited.

Design and editorial by Creative Plus Publishing Ltd,
www.creative-plus.co.uk

Printed and bound in Singapore by Imago

Cover photo by Adam Feery

Bible quotations are from the NIV (New International Version) unless
otherwise stated, included by permission of the International Bible Society.
Bible verses from the CEV (Contemporary English Version) used by
permission of The British and Foreign Bible Society. Bible verses from
the (GNT) Good News Translation used with permission from The Bible
Society. Bible verse from The Message, by Eugene Peterson, published by
Nav Press, used with permission.

The profits from the sale of this book go to support the work of
The Leprosy Mission in hospitals and rehabilitation workshops abroad.
To buy further copies of this book, other Christian books, gifts and cards
telephone 0845 1662253 or shop online at www.tlmtrading.com

For all those who travel through fog,
and struggle to discern God's presence,
and for my amazing family who
walked with me when I was feeling lost
and confused.

And for Megan, who still has a special
place in our hearts.

Travelling through fog

After a long and dreary winter, came one of those stunning days that heralds the arrival of spring. The sun shone out of a clear blue sky and the world seemed a better, brighter place again. Just the sort of day for a long walk on the beach to blow away some winter cobwebs. I began the short drive to the coast, but as I turned to go down the hill that leads to the beach, suddenly great swathes of mist were chasing across the road. By the time I reached the car park, the fog was so dense that it became impossible to see the promenade, sand or sea, despite the fact that they were only metres from the car. Disappointed, I turned around and drove back up the hill towards home.

Once away from the sea, everything was clear, bright and blue again. Later that day, as I reflected on what had happened, I felt the Lord prompt me with a question:

How did you know the sea was still there,
even though you couldn't see it?

My response? Of course the sea was there. It had always been there. Ever since I was a small child I've known it was there. I've watched the waves, paddled in the shallow water, even swum in it on a few rash occasions! Of course it was there. Just because I couldn't see it today didn't mean it wasn't there. A while later, I began to see the point of the question.

There are times on our spiritual journey when 'fog' descends. Often it happens suddenly and without warning. Those around us may still appear to be in glorious sunshine, but we are surrounded by 'fog'. What we once saw with great clarity becomes strangely dim and many of our previous certainties are open to question. We fear that God is no longer with us. In the past, ships lost in foggy seas would search for the beam from the lighthouse to guide them to safety, similarly when 'spiritual fog' descends, we need to seek God's light for guidance, believing that, whilst for a time we may not be able to feel God's presence, He is still with us, and in time the sun will shine for us again too.

My journey began quite unexpectedly, when I found myself struggling with grief and trying to make sense of God's plans. I spent the following two years 'travelling through fog'. In the early days the pain was almost unbearable. Later, pain gave way to frustration and finally I began to see glimpses of hope; the fog beginning to clear.

Your journey may have different origins: depression, redundancy, the loss of a loved one, a broken relationship? Whatever has caused the fog to descend, I pray that in sharing my journey, you may feel less alone as you travel, and that you will emerge stronger, and closer to God.

This book is a collection of reflections gathered along the way. I hope that it will be of some comfort to fellow travellers!

Wendy Grant

Travelling the road of disappointment with God

Now that same day two of them were going to a village called Emmaus, about seven miles from Jerusalem. They were talking with each other about everything that had happened.

LUKE 24:13-14

Most of us have memories of difficult journeys. Those with small children will remember the constant, "Are we nearly there yet?" with 200 miles left to travel! Delays, breakdowns, traffic jams, accidents all make for memorable journeys, albeit for the wrong reasons.

One of the most difficult journeys I have ever made was to deliver an eight-month-old baby to the home of her soon-to-be adoptive parents, knowing that I may never see her again. We had cared for her from birth. She had become like our own daughter and my heart was breaking at the thought of being parted from her. A more difficult journey was the drive home without her, my other children looking on helplessly as I sobbed. However, more challenging still, was the journey yet to come: travelling the road of disappointment with God. Why had He allowed this to happen? Why had He called us into a ministry, which would cause us so much pain? Surely God doesn't make mistakes?

I have no idea how well travelled this road is, since few dare admit they are travelling it. Perhaps we keep quiet for fear that we might be considered lacking in faith, heretical, or weak. Sometimes it is hard to own up to how we are really feeling.

It is encouraging to realise that we are not the first to travel this road. After the crucifixion of Jesus, two disciples, Cleopas and a friend, began walking from Jerusalem to Emmaus, 'their faces downcast'. They had been convinced that Jesus was the Messiah, the one who would redeem Israel and set the Jewish people free from Roman oppression. Then, they had watched him die a cruel death on the cross, and here their disappointment began. They questioned that if Jesus had been God's anointed, surely he would not have died like this? '…we had hoped that he was the one who was going to redeem Israel…' they explain in Luke 24:21; but now their hope is gone, and they are left trying to make sense of their experience. You can read the whole story in Luke 24:13-35.

Lord,
Help me to trust your plan,
even when I don't understand it
and I am in great pain.
Help me to hold on
through the darkness
and wait for the light to dawn.
Amen

We are not alone!

…Jesus himself came up and walked along with them…
LUKE 24:15

One of the most startling and yet comforting discoveries we make on this bewildering journey, is that Jesus himself chooses to walk beside us. Despite the anger and doubt we aim at him, he is faithful to his promise to be with us always (Matthew 28:20).

Like the disciples on the road to Emmaus, our grief and disappointment may keep us from recognising Jesus' presence at first. We may even be reluctant to accept his company, but he remains faithful and committed to us through good times and bad.

If Cleopas and his friend had looked down at Jesus' feet, I'm sure they would have found that his feet too were covered in dust from the road. When Jesus joins us for the journey, it is not in some kind of ethereal bubble. He enters the hardship of our world, the depths of our pain, and chooses to make it his own.

Like the disciples on the road to Emmaus, take time to tell Jesus everything that troubles your heart, all the hurts and disappointments. And thank him for choosing to travel beside you.

....

Lord Jesus,
Though I may not yet be able to recognise your presence with me,
in faith I reach out and take hold of your hand.
Please walk with me through the pain of my disappointment,
until I feel able to trust you again.
Amen

....

Searching for understanding

*"When he talked with us along the road
and explained the Scriptures to us,
didn't it warm our hearts?"*
LUKE 24:32 (CEV)

We do not have the benefit of seeing Jesus physically walking beside us and explaining the scriptures to us, as the Emmaus disciples did. Nor perhaps, will our understanding be as instantaneous as theirs. Paul warns us that, in this world, we may only see things in part (1 Corinthians 13:12).

Sometimes our disappointment springs from an inability to fully grasp God's wider purposes. In that case, we need to commit to reading the Bible diligently, searching its pages and asking God's Spirit to reveal the truth to us. It was not until Jesus 'opened' the Scriptures to Cleopas and his friend, that they were able to understand Jesus' death, in the context of God's plan for the redemption of mankind. Previously they had thought that, either they had been wrong in believing Jesus was the Messiah, or worse, that God had made a mistake in allowing Jesus to die. Once understanding dawns, they are no longer 'downcast', but re-energised and re-focused.

Returning to the fog analogy, years ago many ships would have run aground in dense fog, if they hadn't sought the beam from the lighthouse to guide them to safety. So it is on our spiritual journey. When we hit dense 'spiritual fog' we have to commit to careful searching, so that God in His grace and mercy can show us the way to keep on course, and allow us to see things in their proper context.

Your word is a lamp to my feet and a light to my path.
PSALM 119:105

Lord God,
By your Spirit would you open the Scriptures to me,
as you did to the disciples on the road to Emmaus.
Please help me to understand what I'm going through
in the context of your greater plans.
Help me in my confusion not to stray from the right path.
Amen

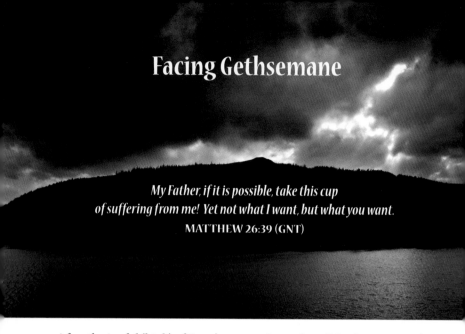

Facing Gethsemane

*My Father, if it is possible, take this cup
of suffering from me! Yet not what I want, but what you want.*
MATTHEW 26:39 (GNT)

After the joyful 'high' of Jesus' entry to Jerusalem (Matthew 21:1-11), after the power and passion of the Temple clearance (Matthew 21:12 and 13) and after the agony of farewells at the Last Supper (Matthew 26:17-30), now Jesus faces the desperation of Gethsemane.

In that garden, the plan for the salvation of the world was being contested. The battle of bringing the human will in line with the divine was raging. We will never fully understand the depths of agony and loneliness Jesus suffered there.

Jesus confides in his disciples, "*My soul is overwhelmed with sorrow to the point of death.*" (Matthew 26:38). Such was his anguish; he felt it was possible that he might even die right there in the garden. Luke's version of this event tells us that, Jesus' sweat was like 'drops of blood falling to the ground' (Luke 22:44), as he battled with the prospect of the cross.

This was no ordinary decision-making process!

Perhaps you have had moments of wishing you could die too? Each of us, at some time in our journey through life, may face our own private 'Gethsemane'; intolerable grief, crushing disappointment, desperate loneliness. In the darkness, we too may need to battle; to be able to say to our Father God, as Jesus did, "Yet not as I will, but as you will."(Matthew 26:39)

We may need to learn to submit our human will to God's, even though we don't understand, and don't know how we will find the strength to carry on. In that moment, we will probably feel utterly alone. Our friends may well be 'sleeping', leaving us feeling overwhelmed with sorrow. We need to remember that Jesus has been there before us; that he has already fought the battle and won it on our behalf, and that it is His strength that will guide us through.

....

Lord Jesus,
There are times when I am overwhelmed with sorrow,
to the point of death.
I don't know how to carry on with life.
In those moments,
I confess that I don't always want what you want,
and battle to bring my will into line with yours.
Help me to remember Gethsemane:
to acknowledge the agonies you suffered there,
and to be thankful that, because you fought and overcame,
I can trust you to strengthen me,
and enable me to overcome in my hour of darkness.
Loving Lord Jesus, thank you.
Amen
....

The agony of the cross

About the ninth hour Jesus cried out in a loud voice,
"Eloi, Eloi, Lama sabachthani?" which means,
"My God, my God why have you forsaken me?"
MATTHEW 27:46

Many suggest that Jesus was quoting Psalm 22 here, because that Psalm begins with the same words, '*Why have you forsaken me?*', but ends with triumph and praise. Yet William Barclay, in his commentary on Matthew's gospel, suggests that in the agony of the cross, one would hardly recite poetry, not even the poetry of a Psalm. I don't know if he's right but perhaps we prefer to think that Jesus was quoting Psalm 22, because we are uncomfortable with the notion that, at this point, Jesus felt utterly abandoned.

However, in rushing desperately to the place of triumph, we overlook a crucial moment: as Jesus cries out to his Father, "Why have you forsaken me?", he is weighed down, not just with physical and emotional pain, but with the spiritual pain of separation from his Father. On the cross, in order to secure our salvation, Jesus took on himself the weight of the entire world's sin and evil, and thus experienced the deepest suffering possible and the blackest darkness. And, because Jesus himself experienced those depths, He understands how it feels!

In those times when we feel utterly alone, when we might feel that even our Father has deserted us, Jesus is right there in the midst of our suffering; he has felt that pain too. Because of the cross, there is no depth to which we descend that Jesus has not already experienced.

Dear Lord Jesus,
Thank you that because of your death on the cross,
you understand those moments when I feel utterly abandoned.
Thank you that there are no depths of suffering unknown to you.
Thank you that you were willing to suffer and die for me.
Please help me to find a way through this pain.
Amen

Facing our brokenness

…and as she stood behind him at his feet weeping, she began to wet his feet with her tears.
LUKE 7:38

On the walls of our local swimming baths are several mosaics. One of them is a picture of a dancer and a dolphin. It is stunning, but I have to confess that it is only recently that I have studied it in any detail. The dolphin is made of regular shaped pieces of beautifully coloured ceramics; all except for its belly, which is made of razor-sharp shards of mirrors.

During the past few months my pain and brokenness has been razor sharp. I have not known how to trust God for the future. I have been unable to see how he could bring anything positive out of my experience. Can I believe that my heartache, when placed into God's hands, may produce something beautiful?

Studying this dolphin mosaic gives me hope. Hope that, whilst I can't see it yet, one day I will be able to understand that my life is like a hand-crafted mosaic; one in which God has been able to use all the pieces, even the razor-sharp ones, to make something beautiful.

Lord Jesus,
Help me to offer you my tears and brokenness, as Mary did,
and to trust you to make something beautiful with them,
just as you did for her.
Amen

More travelling companions

Now faith is being sure of what we hope for and certain of what we do not see.
This is what the ancients were commended for.

HEBREWS 11:1-2

Many of those named by Paul as great men of faith, in Hebrews
chapters 11 and 12, had travelled through 'fog'. When we read about
the lives of Noah, Abraham, Joseph, Moses and others, we see not
only moments of great faith and triumph, but also, moments of
intense doubt and uncertainty.

Noah is asked by God to build an enormous ark, long before so much
as a rain cloud appears (Genesis 6:9-22). There must have been times
when Noah wondered about God's plans for him – most especially
after many months in a large ocean-going vessel where he was
completely surrounded by water and smelly animals!

God told **Abraham** that he would have offspring as numerous as the
stars (Genesis 15:5), but many, many years later, he was still waiting
for a single child.

In a dream, God revealed to **Joseph**, that one day he would be
someone of great importance, and that others would bow down
to him, but he was sold into slavery and later wrongly imprisoned
(Genesis 37:5-7).

What sets these men apart, is not necessarily their ultimate success,
but their ability to persevere; to press on, believing that, no matter
how awful things appear, ultimately God is in control. For each of
them, the fruitful years did eventually come, and each was rewarded
for his faith. For us too, the challenge is to remain faithful in difficult

times, when nothing seems to make sense; choosing to hold on to our belief that God is ultimately in control, and persevering in the hope that the fruitful years will come to us also.

L ord,
There are days when nothing seems to make sense
and I feel as if I'm holding on to faith by the tips of my finger-nails.
Help me to remember that I am in good company.
Help me to keep hope alive,
to keep believing that the fruitful years will come,
and to keep trusting in your goodness.
Amen

God's hidden purpose

But God sent me on ahead of you to keep your families
alive and to save you in this wonderful way.
GENESIS 45:7 (CEV)

In the Bible, the story of Jacob's son, Joseph, is long and complicated. It begins in Genesis 37 and concludes in Genesis 50, after many years and many twists and turns in his fortunes.

Joseph's life is one of contrasts: favoured son – hated brother; rescued from death – sold into slavery; trusted servant – wrongfully imprisoned; powerful Governor – vulnerable brother, and son.

There must have been occasions when Joseph was bewildered by the circumstances of his life. As he languished in prison for several years, he too must have had times of being frightened and confused. How had he ended up here? Why had his brothers betrayed him so cruelly? And where was God?

Perhaps like us, Joseph struggled to see how anything good could possibly come from his trials. Maybe he questioned God's promises. But to his credit, despite incredible hardship and persecution, Joseph was able to hold on to his faith, and emerge as a man free from bitterness, reconciled to God's purposes. Many years later, when Joseph was finally reunited with his brothers, he says, *"Do not be distressed and do not be angry with yourselves for selling me here, because it was to save lives that God sent me ahead of you."* (Genesis 45:5)

It takes great courage and faith to try to recognise God's purposes in the midst of personal suffering, so that our lives are marked by grace, not bitterness. We may find it frustrating that often God's plans remain hidden from us for prolonged periods of time.

For Joseph, circumstances changed suddenly and unexpectedly, and God's purposes were revealed. In our lives too, the unexpected may be just around the corner, if we wait expectantly for the Lord. As we look back over our lives, hopefully we too will detect God's hand at work, in ways that we didn't initially recognise, gradually bringing to completion His master plan.

And even if we cannot yet see God's purposes unfolding in our own life, perhaps we can take heart that one day soon, there will come a 'But God…' (Genesis 45:7) moment, just as there was for Joseph.

....

Dear Lord,
In this moment of darkness,
it is hard to perceive your purposes.
Please give me the faith to believe
that you are at work in some hidden way
and that some good will come out of my
present troubles.
Amen

....

Tears

He has sent me to bind up the broken-hearted…
to comfort all who mourn…
to bestow on them a crown of beauty instead
of ashes, the oil of gladness instead of
mourning…
ISAIAH 61:1-3

For some time after our little foster baby left us, a frequent refrain was heard in our house, "Pass Mum a tissue someone!" However, walking to school with my little girl one day, I realised that I wasn't the only one to be affected by the loss. "Mummy," she said, in an unusually quiet voice. "You know I'm not crying about this very much? It's because on the surface I'm fine. It's deep down it hurts." You may find that you are unable to cry, but deep down it hurts. Or, like me, you may have had days when you can't believe there could be any more tears left to cry, and then you cry some more!

There are many verses in the Bible that remind us that our sadness will not last forever. When we read these words, we can be encouraged that one day our tears will give way to joy. I am looking forward to that special day of rejoicing, when all my tears are wiped away.

....

Father God,
Thank you that our tears are not unnoticed.
Thank you for the promises in your Word,
that reassure me that a time of restoration will come.
I long for the 'oil of gladness instead of mourning'.
Help me to keep trusting you.
Amen

....

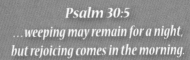

Psalm 30:5
…weeping may remain for a night,
but rejoicing comes in the morning.

Psalm 126:5
Those who sow in tears
will reap with songs of joy.

Isaiah 25:8
The Sovereign LORD will wipe away the
tears from all faces…

Revelation 21:4
He will wipe every tear from their eyes.
There will be no more death or mourning or crying or pain.
for the old order of things has passed away.

The Father's heart

But while he was still a long way off, his father saw him and was filled with compassion for him; he ran to his son, threw his arms around him and kissed him.
LUKE 15:20

It remains a wonderful mystery to me that, in the depths of our pain as we begin searching for answers, the Lord graciously reveals to us glimpses of things that we could not previously have understood.

Some weeks after our foster baby had moved on, I was visiting a local Church for a united service. Whilst waiting for the service to begin, I scanned the unfamiliar surroundings. This church was full of ornate stonework. I noticed above me, a little carving of a cherub, with tears on its face. My stomach knotted as it had done frequently in the previous days and I contemplated an awful question once again. What if she's crying and I'm not there to comfort her?

That night I found it difficult to sleep. In my diary I wrote these words.

> *What if you should cry and I'm not there to comfort you?*
> *What if you should fall and I'm not there to hold you?*
> *What if you should laugh and I'm not there to laugh with you?*
> *What if you were to discover something new and I am not there to share it with you?*
> *And what if you should return...?*

As I finished writing, I thought of the story that Jesus told about the returning prodigal and the extravagant party his father ordered to celebrate his return. I am probably the world's biggest 'party pooper',

but I knew without a doubt, that if somehow our baby were to return, we would throw the biggest party ever! And in that moment, I believe I understood, as never before, our Father God's aching heart for His lost children.

There were times when I ached physically as well as emotionally, longing to hold our baby again. If I, so imperfect and frail, could feel such pain for a child not even born to me, what depths of pain must our Father God feel for his children: those whom He has known since the beginning of time, created and brought into being.
'Before I formed you in the womb, I knew you, before you were born I set you apart…' (Jeremiah 1:5).

Our heavenly Father loves each one of us 'truly, madly, deeply', and aches for those who are lost.

. . . .

Heavenly Father,
Thank you that in the midst of our darkness, you shine your light, and impart new depths of understanding.
Thank you that you love your children so passionately.
Amen

. . . .

The Father's compassion

The day is nearly over.
The sun is beginning to set; the light fading.
A man stands alone on a balcony, looking out.
This is not the first time.
He has done this every day for as long as he can remember.
His heart is heavy, waiting, longing,
aching for the return of his beloved child.
He strains to see into the distance, his eyes scanning the horizon.
The landscape is dry and empty;
as it has been every other night he's stood here.
But still he waits.
He looks first one way, and then another,
standing on tiptoe, leaning out.
Nothing.
Nobody.
His heart sinks again.
As another day ends, he begins to turn away, slowly, reluctantly;
hope fading with the light.
But as he turns, he catches a glimpse of dust rising,
way out in the distance.
His heart begins to race. Could it be…?
Is this the moment he's longed for?
Then, hope gives way to anxiety.
What if it's just a weary traveller passing through?
Could this be another crushing disappointment?
He is compelled to find out.

Meanwhile, a figure is trudging slowly along the dusty road.
Dejected, head down, rehearsing a speech.
'I'm not worthy. I'm not worthy...'
He looks up momentarily and sees clouds of dust.
Someone, or something, is rushing towards him.
He is gripped with fear,
then suddenly, caught up in a powerful embrace.
The traveller falls to his knees and hides his face.
"Father, I'm not worthy," he begins. "I'm not worthy… "
But his words are covered in an embrace.
"My child, welcome," is the Father's reply.

Heavenly Father,
I long to feel the extravagance of your love
and the warmth of your embrace.
Please help me to find my way back to you.
Amen

Choosing to worship

By the rivers of Babylon we sat and wept...
How can we sing the songs of the LORD
while in a foreign land?

PSALM 137:1 & 4

Just as I was beginning my journey through 'fog', a song by Matt and Beth Redman, 'Blessed be your name', became very popular at our Church.

> *You give and take away, You give and take away.*
> *My heart will choose to say, Lord, blessed be your name.*

I decided that the only people who could really sing those words, were those who had never lost anyone, or anything. I resolved that I could not sing it. I confess that at that moment, I could not summon the strength to bless the Lord.

It was some months, before I realised that worship is a choice, not necessarily a feeling. In our state of deep loss, we might not *feel* like blessing the Lord, but we can *choose* to do so. In making that choice, we take a step towards acknowledging the sovereignty of God.

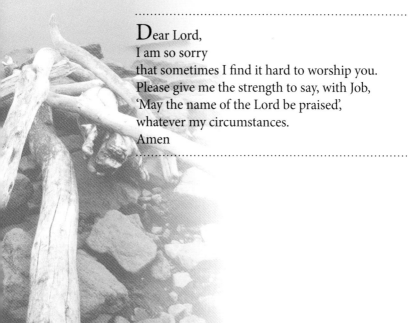

Also, in making the choice to worship, even when it's difficult, we offer the Lord a costly sacrifice of praise, and can say with King David, that we will not sacrifice that which cost us nothing (1 Chronicles 21:24). I have come to believe that such worship is precious to the Lord.

If you are finding it difficult to worship, take a moment to reflect on feelings and choices. Ask the Lord to help you find the strength to begin to worship Him in some way, despite your circumstances.

The song, 'Blessed be your name', is based on Job 1:21: 'The LORD gave and the LORD has taken away; May the name of the LORD be praised.' Job endured so much and yet he still made a conscious decision to worship God. Sometimes we need to start worshipping, whether we want to or not, then slowly the desire to worship wells up.

....

Dear Lord,
I am so sorry
that sometimes I find it hard to worship you.
Please give me the strength to say, with Job,
'May the name of the Lord be praised',
whatever my circumstances.
Amen

....

Permission to lament

My God, my God, why have you abandoned me?
PSALM 22:1 (GNT)

Have you ever noticed how many of the Psalms begin, not with acclamations of praise, but with cries of anguish or despair? Psalm 22, is perhaps one of the most famous of these.

These expressions of anguish and despair could have been 'air-brushed' out of Scripture to give its pages a more positive glow, but I'm so glad they weren't. Instead, the book of Psalms shows us a pattern of worship that gives us the opportunity to be real before God; to express our confusion, hurt, or even anger with Him.

This permission to lament is vital to a healthy relationship with God and to our ability to worship. If we do not allow it, we run the risk of encouraging pretence, which is both dangerous and unrealistic. For most of us, life is not an uninterrupted succession of triumphs. In difficult times, we need to feel that we can cry out to God without feeling a failure. We also need to bear in mind that there is little point in pretence before God; He already knows our hearts.

Within individual Psalms, we often see a move from anguish to praise or reaffirmation of God's goodness. Again, Psalm 22 is a good example of this. Although it begins with a cry of despair, by verse 5 the writer is calling to mind examples of God's faithfulness, and by verse 23 he is calling on all those who fear the Lord to praise him!

The pattern of worship in many of our churches gives little room for lament. But, if in private we are able to adopt the Psalmist's model of

openness before God, hopefully, we too will eventually break through into the assurance of God's presence, remembrance of his deliverance, and ultimately, into songs of praise.

Lord God,
When worship is difficult, help me to remember
that the Psalms give me permission to lament first.
Thank you for allowing me to be honest with you,
and for always loving me.
Amen

Re-building the altar

... and he repaired the altar of the LORD, which was in ruins.

1 KINGS 18:30

The account of the contest on Mount Carmel between Elijah and the prophets of Baal is well known (1 Kings 18:20-46). It is remembered and quoted for many different reasons: the triumph of God over the prophets of Baal, an example of true faith, and so on. A lone prophet of Yahweh takes on hundreds of prophets of Baal and wins! However, until recently, I had missed what I now consider to be a really important part of the account in the book of Kings. Verses 30 to 32 record how, before Elijah was able to prepare the sacrifice, he had to re-build the altar of the Lord.

During the reign of King Ahab, many of the altars built specifically for making sacrifices to the Lord, had been neglected, or even torn down and replaced with altars to other gods. To me, Elijah's re-building is a hugely significant act, symbolising the restoration of God's rightful place.

As we 'travel through fog,' we may find that our trust in God is eroded, or our view of Him diminished. We may also have allowed other things to take His place. It is possible therefore, that we too may have some 're-building' work to do, before we can enter into sacrificial worship.

Almighty God,
I confess that my pain and confusion have caused me
to lose sight of how great and mighty you are.
I have allowed my view of you to become diminished,
and my worship impoverished.
Lord, please forgive me
and help me to restore you
to your rightful place in my life.
Amen

Maps and timetables

So God led the people…
EXODUS 13:18

In my daily Bible notes, I once read that God doesn't give advance copies of His perfect timetable. I'd like to add that He doesn't give us a map either!

When God called Moses to lead His people out of slavery in Egypt, (Exodus 3:1-10), He gave no indication of how long their journey would take, or by what road they were to travel. Details were scarce. He promised only that He was taking them to a better place; 'a good and spacious land, a land flowing with milk and honey…' (Exodus 3:8). The moment that the Israelites left the familiarity of Egypt, we see that their journey was not going to be straightforward.

'*God did not lead them on the road through the Philistine country, though that was shorter…So God led the people around by the desert road towards the Red Sea*' (Exodus 13:17 and 18).

Often, when 'fog' falls, we feel as if we are wandering with no destination in sight and possibly no timescale to work to. It can be hugely frustrating. However, God was there, *leading* the Israelites.

He even sent a pillar of cloud by day and a pillar of fire by night to guide them and enable them to travel at any time. God had planned the way meticulously. He knew exactly what they needed to learn and experience. Although it may have appeared to the Israelites that they were wandering aimlessly, God had charge of both the map and the timetable. During this time of waiting and

wandering, the Israelites were being prepared by God to be marked as His holy people, in the land of their inheritance.

As we make our own journey through life, the way may often seem long and convoluted to us. We may be tempted to give up and chose an easier path; in fact the Israelites were often tempted to do just that. But I am beginning to realise that we need to trust that God has a direction, and destination in mind for us, too. In order for us to reach that destination, we may need to spend some time being prepared, and 'travelling through fog' may be an important part of that preparation.

D ear Lord,
Help me to trust you, even when I can't
see the map or the timetable.
Help me also to be open to the work of
preparation you may need to do in my life.
Amen

Show me your ways, O Lord, teach me your paths…

PSALM 25:4

A time of searching

To you, O LORD, I lift up my soul; in you I trust, O my God.
Show me your ways, O LORD, teach me your paths; guide me
in your truth and teach me, for you are God my Saviour, and
my hope is in you all day long.
All the ways of the LORD are loving and faithful for those
who keep the demands of his covenant.
My eyes are ever on the LORD, for only he will release my feet
from the snare.

PSALM 25, VERSES 1, 4, 5, 10 & 15

Browsing through my prayer journals one day, I was surprised to find that in periods when life was going well, I had made far fewer entries, than in these difficult days of uncertainty. I realised that in the darkness, I was craving God's light. Just as a flower reaches for the sun, so I was reaching for understanding through reading the Bible.

On one occasion, I read Psalm 25. The words reminded me that when the time was right, the Lord would reveal the way ahead. I also became aware that I needed to renew my trust that He is willing and able to guide me.

As I continued reading through the psalm, I wondered about the phrase 'my hope is in you all day long'. Disappointment and grief had eroded my hope. I needed to re-establish that sense of hope, based on a rightful relationship with God.

Then, I became deeply aware that my eyes had not been 'ever on the Lord'. I needed to confess that, and lift my eyes heavenwards once more. Finally, I had to consider whether there were any 'snares' that were holding back my progress on the journey, remembering that, 'only He', is able to release us. Perhaps you are aware that you need to take similar steps today.

....

Heavenly Father,
Thank you that when our eyes are on you,
you will reveal the way ahead.
Help us to renew our trust in you
and restore in us a sense of hope for the future.
And Father, where there are 'snares',
please release us from them,
so that we can walk in the paths you have chosen for us.
Amen

....

Desert experiences

Jesus, full of the Holy Spirit, returned from the Jordan and was led by the Spirit in the desert...

LUKE 4:1

I have often heard this experience of 'travelling through fog', likened to a 'desert time'. It takes courage to enter the desert, because in the desert nothing is familiar and nothing seems to flourish; the landscape is always the same, shifting sand, making it hard to find the way. In the desert, the Israelites were learning utter dependence on God and to follow God's leading (Numbers 9:15-23). It took them 40 years!

Jesus also went into the desert, and again we learn that He was not abandoned; on the contrary, He 'was led by the Spirit' (Luke 4:1). In our own desert times, I am beginning to realise that God is teaching us to be utterly dependent on Him, and sends His Spirit to guide us.

During a Church weekend away, a few of us took part in a Biblical meditation, focusing on Psalm 139. I had been reluctant to go on that weekend away. 'Travelling through fog' can be a very isolating

experience. However, as the second day drew to a close, and we reflected on this Psalm together, I was very glad to be there because the opening words spoke to me deeply... 'O Lord, you have searched me and you know me.'

All the time that I had been grappling with uncertainties, I had been searching for God. Now, as I read these verses, I realised that while I was searching for Him, so He had been searching my heart; perceiving my thoughts and anxieties. The 'desert' it seems, is a place of double searching; us after God, and Him after us. In the desert God searches our hearts, pin-points those things that need dealing with, and prepares us for future service.

....

Father God,
Thank you that you do not abandon us in our 'desert' times.
Thank you that as we search for you, you also are searching our hearts; making us ready for the next stage of our lives.
Help us to learn to depend on you more and more.
Amen

....

Stuck at Good Friday

But after I am raised to life,
I will go ahead of you to Galilee.
MARK 14:28 (CEV)

One Sunday morning, during the worship time at Church, I considered the smiling, radiant faces of the worship leaders and felt very aggrieved. "It's all right for them, Lord," I moaned, "some of us are in pain." Then, I sensed the Lord reply, "Wendy, the trouble is, you're stuck at Good Friday."

Initially, I was even more aggrieved by this response, but as I reflected on it, I realised how true it was. My experience of 'travelling through fog' had taught me so much about the agony of Gethsemane; of costly obedience, of sacrifice and suffering. But actually I was in danger of being stuck there and failing to see beyond the pain to the joy of the resurrection.

After the Last Supper, Jesus said to His disciples, "But after I have risen, I will go ahead of you into Galilee." (Matthew 26:32). Despite the agonies that lay ahead, Jesus was able to look beyond the cross to the glorious day of Resurrection. There is a famous phrase, which is often quoted in Easter sermons, "It may be Friday, but Sunday is coming." In other words, if we are stuck at Good Friday, in the pain and suffering, we need to remember that Resurrection Sunday is coming!

Dear Lord Jesus,
Thank you that beyond the desperation of the cross,
was the joy of the resurrection morning.
Please help me to look beyond my present circumstances,
trusting that joy will come.
Amen

Prayers of new hope

After the darkness of winter, comes the brightness of spring.
Lord, thank you for spring time.

After the darkness of the crucifixion, came the light of the resurrection.
Lord, be with me in my darkness, may I soon experience your light.

After the agony of the cross, came restoration and new life.
Lord, I am in pain, and long for restoration and wholeness.

After the despair of watching Jesus die, came the joy of seeing him live again.
Lord, when I feel desperate, help me believe that joy will come.

After separation from God, came the chance to enter his presence.
Lord, even when I feel far from you, please stay close to me.

After Jesus died, he rose to life again,
Lord, help me to trust you for a new beginning.

Amen

Photo: Lydia Grant

The coming of spring

I am the true vine, and my Father is the gardener
JOHN 15:1

The Lord speaks to us in many different ways. Recently I read
The Secret Garden, by Frances Hodgson Burnett, with one of our
daughters. It's a delightful story, in which a little orphan girl, Mary
Lennox, discovers and secretly tends a long-neglected garden,
together with her friend Dickon. There is a poignant moment when
Mary takes Dickon into the garden for the first time. It is still winter,
the garden is grey and cold. Mary is afraid that the garden is 'quite
dead'. But Dickon expertly cuts away at seemingly dead wood to show

her that, even when things seem dead, if there is the tiniest bit of green, it means that at the right time the roses will blossom. "There'll be a fountain o' roses here this summer," he says.

I read this at a time when I was feeling sad and frustrated that, as a result of my spiritual 'fog', there didn't seem to be much 'blossoming' in my life. Like little Mary, I was concerned that everything seemed 'quite dead'. However, I believe the Lord used this story to reawaken in me a hope that, just as in nature things are not necessarily dead, merely waiting for the right time to blossom, so it is in our spiritual lives.

In times of crisis, many areas of our lives shut down, in order to cope with our immediate situation. Far from being dead, there is a major work going on beneath us at root level. A work which, though often imperceptible, is vital in re-establishing our ability to hold firm and bloom at the right time.

In John 15:1, Jesus tells us that his Father is the gardener. We need to have confidence therefore, that The Master Gardener will know how to tend our needs, in order for new growth to appear.

While the spring is still a little way off for me, and perhaps for you too, I am increasingly hopeful that it will come soon!

Arise, my darling,
my beautiful one, and come with me.
See! The winter is past;
the rains are over and gone.
Flowers appear on the earth;
the season of singing has come…
SONG OF SONGS 2:10-12

Leaving the fog behind

*Please give us this land as our property, and do not make us
cross the Jordan River and settle there.*

NUMBERS 32:5 (GNT)

We thought previously about how it takes courage to enter the desert.
I am now learning that it also takes courage to leave it and move on
with our lives.

It alarmed me to realise that, having begun my journey through
fog, 'kicking and screaming' so to speak, I was now reluctant for the
journey to end. I had begun to enjoy the solitude with God and was
aware that, for this journey to finish, and for me to move on to new
things, there needed to be an end to this intense and intimate time of
discovery. And yet, to fail to take steps to move on, would mean the
risk of missing out on the future God had prepared.

In Numbers 32, we read that some of the Israelites had become
comfortable where they were. Although they were willing to fight
with the other Israelite tribes to secure the Promised Land, they did
not want to inhabit it. They preferred to stay where there was good
grazing land. This side of eternity we can never know for sure, but I
wonder if they didn't settle for comfort, rather than risk moving on to
discover their full inheritance on the other side of the Jordan.

Similarly, I am aware that the time may be coming when God beckons
me to take fresh steps of faith and begin a new journey. Perhaps you
feel that you still have further to travel on your present journey. But
the right time will come for each of us when God will want to lead us
onwards, out of the fog, back into the sunshine.

He has plans prepared for us and plans that he has been preparing us for. In God's economy nothing is wasted. Even our painful experiences can be turned into positives for Him.

For me, taking steps of faith has involved exploring a sense of God calling us to become an adoptive family. When the time is right, God will have a new journey, a new calling, a new adventure ready for you too.

Heavenly Father,
It took courage to begin this journey, but now I am discovering that it also takes courage to move on.
Father, at the right time, would you enable me
to sense your calling and give me the ability to respond.
Amen

The victor's cry

It is finished.
JOHN 19:30

On the cross, the work of redemption was accomplished. The agony was over, the task completed, the battle won, sin and death defeated for all time. Jesus' cries of abandonment give way to the ultimate statement of completion, "It is finished."

We too have the opportunity to shout the victor's cry, if we can continue to cling to the fragments of faith we have left, and refuse to let go of God. We may descend to the depths, but because of Jesus, we can also one day soar to the heights of heaven.

Lord God,
Thank you that if I cling to you,
your light will eventually break through
into my darkness.
Thank you that because of Jesus' victory on the cross,
I can look forward with joy, to eternity with you.
Amen

Breaking through!

The moon will be as bright as the sun, and the sun will be seven times brighter than usual, like the light of seven days in one. This will all happen when the Lord bandages and heals the wounds he has given his people.
ISAIAH 30:26 (GNT)

Today, our soon-to-be adopted daughter came to our house for the first time. Months ago, she had asked social workers for a new mummy and daddy who would take her to the beach and to the park. So, this afternoon we took her to the beach, to play on the sand and watch the waves. There was no fog, only sunshine.

Our prayer for our new daughter, and all adopted children, is that they will one day come to know our awesome heavenly Father, who can be trusted with their pain, and who commits to walk with them through the sunshine and the fog.

There is of course a sense in which God wants to personally adopt each of his children into his own family.

"Long, long ago he decided to adopt us into his family through Jesus Christ. (What pleasure he took in planning this!)" (Ephesians 1:5, *The Message*).

I am aware that as one journey ends, another is beginning. Once again, I need to place my hand in God's hand and trust Him for all that lies ahead.

*Now to him who is able to do immeasurably more than all
we ask or imagine, according to his power that is at work
within us, to him be glory in the Church and in Christ
Jesus, throughout all generations, forever and ever! Amen.*

EPHESIANS 3:20-21

This Bible reference is engraved on the inside of my wedding ring,
which confused the engraver who was expecting the name of a
person! It's a reminder to me that, despite my failures and weaknesses,
and my periods of uncertainty, God is able to do immeasurably more
than I can ask or even imagine.

I hope that wherever you are on your journey of faith, you will begin
to see more and more of His power at work in your life, and that we
will each increasingly trust Him for all our tomorrows.